Starlight & ERROR

REMICA BINGHAM-RISHER

Winner of the Diode Editions Book Award

Copyright ©Remica Bingham-Risher
First Edition 2017
All rights reserved.

ISBN: 978-1-939728-10-4
Diode Editions
Doha, Qatar

Design & layout: Law Alsobrook
Cover art: *Arms Are For Holding*, Deborah Shedrick ©2014
Author photo: Rachel Eliza Griffiths

Ordering & Contact information: http://www.diodeeditions.com

For my husband: I'm singing this song to you.

Imagine your first love as a road of crumbs
marking a path back to the awakened whole

and your future
as all the small, invisible hungers of this world

—Julia Levine

I

11 Benediction
12 If It's Magic
13 Junior Bee v. Sweet Dee: First Sight, Fort Monmouth Pool, 1978
14 Distant Lover (Dear Shirley)
15 Young, small and growing, often violently
16 Cleaning House
17 Delicious, New Edition, 1986
18 Distant Lover (Dear Bobby)
19 The Flock of Your Pasture
21 Domestic
23 We Argue in Silence
24 Mary Robbins Dies 12 Days After Her Husband

II

29 Conduit
30 My Aunt Kisses Jackie Wilson
31 Love In Stereo
32 Vinyl
33 Scene
34 Getting Ready for the Heartache to Come or A Body Intercepting Light
35 Lactation Room
36 How I Knew Michael
37 *Regents Prompt: What are the best ways for step-parents to deal with the special problems they face?*
38 East River Drive
39 The Lift

III

43 Counsel, Wedding Day
45 Equal Measure
47 Fast Car
49 We Awaken Near the Ocean After Being Married
50 Son · sor · éa (\sahn-soar-ray\)
52 Ways to Please a Five-year-old Superhero
53 Baby Be Mine
54 Noble & Webster, Shadow Sculptures
55 Solstice
56 Skipping Stones

IV

61 Training or a Weapon
62 On Religion
63 Photograph
64 Our child is not yet ten and we are clearing his closet
65 We See *The Lion King* on Broadway, I Enter the Pride
66 Some Sorrow, Some Joy
68 A student writes the thesis: *If you never find your soulmate, this is when one must face the harsh reality of making major decisions alone* and, though the grammar is incorrect, I give him credit
69 If this world is ending
70 Beckoning
71 Mother Necessity
72 To Her Whose Heart Is My Heart's Quiet Home
73 Starlight Park

Notes
Acknowledgments

I

Benediction

Bless my parents—impractical anomaly—divorcing when I'm twelve, remarrying when I'm twenty. Bless my aunt and uncle who harbored my parents before me, then held fast, too, these forty odd years. Bless our exemplars, motley kin from which we're birthed: wives, seed, saplings and all living in the same dirt. Let the dogwood tree of time—sublime in tending the soldiers and flames, bearing boughs for each walk of life: rollerskates, the altar, fever and the crucifix lie—be evergreen, four-leafed and golden-centered. Bless the boys who loved us before they were forced to be men. Bless the girls grown out of women. Let the children learn early: people are only as powerful as you let them be. Let the fools who couldn't love us—like the astronomer loves the dark matter he'll never see, like night trains love Georgia and distance disappearing, like the wound loves the cells reborn after suturing—be chaff in the wind of our wandering. Bless love stronger than pride and flesh wounds. Bless the body rising in spite of itself. Let the rites passed down—*love until it hurts, love like you'll be living forever, love like what ails you will heal*—be the red unsown, a temple burning. Let the beloved be free or always returning.

If It's Magic

When I find the *Songs in the Key of Life* 45s
I marvel at the messages my parents inscribed:

Sweet Dee and Junior Bee—In Love '79
their marks on the sheath's concentric circles,

inside, on the lyrics booklet, worn smooth
their scratches on the grooves.

I spend a year playing the set
enthralled every few days by some new epithet—

a background voice trailing,
a tone's shift or timbre—

my mother counts the years since their beginning,
how I interrupt their ending,

heartache and revelry,
what each of us remembers.

Such strange obsessions I inherit:
their soulful cinders, indecipherable

refrains, this awful insistence
on fraught and ordinary pain.

Junior Bee v. Sweet Dee
First Sight, Fort Monmouth Pool, 1978

What was spinning?	Everything touched by my gold smile,
It's cliché to say *Brick House*, but it was	turning, again, curious and calling out.
she walked by and I fell in love.	I didn't notice him but he says he saw
Those full lips and that yellow two-piece,	me in my swimsuit; remembers the butterflies too
I ſtill dream of her in it,	years later when we are married,
ſtanding there, too scared to jump in.	long before we have you.
Bobby had to hold her hand.	Shirley was near the edge with the boys.
We were moſtly children then	Never did learn to swim. All of us—
singing and jiving, pretending.	what taxed percussion, our collision.
Who knew what was outside those doors?	I was fine and he was probably spoken for.
If I'd have guessed what would come—	Spirit driving us to
countless records and cities, impatient arms—	the rushed affair behind the house
maybe I wouldn't have followed her,	where we both swore. If I
found her picture in a familiar place,	heard the ſtroke of caution
a beaming ornament. I might have	—swift and ſteady like a walking bass line—
imagined all I could lose, but she was the one	he held us together with his tender certainty
that much I knew.	

Distant Lover

Dear Shirley: They sent us somewhere else I can't mention.
If I disappear, I guess they'll tell you where we been.

Might as well be another planet, air so thick
it's like we're learning to breathe again.

We see things in the trees when nothing's there.
No one admits it but we're scared

of what we left behind.
On recon, walking point, everybody's jumpy—

white boys acting funny, Agent Orange getting into Bloods—
they keep saying the war's over but the world

ain't changed that much. The other night we saw
some boys as small as ours turned to nothing in the road.

No one knows where mines are scattered.
All our time is borrowed.

I been thinking about that night we met at Bob's Lounge.
You, in that thigh high dress and me, gone with one glance.

You stood up slow and easy, pulling everybody's strings.
Over here, guys want to forget everything, be left alone.

You remind me I want to be alive for something.
I'll call when we get orders home.

Young, small and growing, often violently

Music can't save you but it marks a place
        and the knife can be a fierce negotiator.

I learn this reckoning from the women raising me:
        my mother's four sisters, my father's three,

grandmothers, play cousins, surrogate aunties.
        They crowd the table, throwing cards and customs,

warbling. I take a shining to everything
        they allow me to hear—*The Wiz*!

and Kingdom Melodies, Motown, Handel,
        every haunt and opening.

They tell me singing is my gift, use it
        for rapture *not* apology,

and to cut any boy who messes with me.
        At weddings, funerals, school assemblies—

my voice is their tender yield.
        Boys brave enough to try me

always learn what I'm learning to be:
        a straight blade, a canticle, bigger

than their scattering, curve and contour
        of mothers' hands, echo,

aurora, an orchestra,
        a galaxy.

Cleaning House

There is a moment in her life when my Aunt curses and rants in the name of God, uses hands and knees to abandon prayer, and turns to scrubbing boards for salvation. Her husband, covetous fool that he is, has taken up with Ms. Karen, a married woman who lives in the cul-de-sac two streets away. Karen has watched my Aunt's children, brought her paper to the door, pledged friendship, fine print in hand. After she has entered my Uncle fiercely—sliced through his stomach with a kitchen knife—we find my Aunt, clutching a sponge and old bucket, on her knees, scrubbing carpet like she is bringing sandpaper to rough wood. *There's blood on the floor*, she says, and doesn't rise, though we explain the police are waiting and the children have been loaded into a safe woman's car. I been to her house, she says, the Brillo from the sponge cutting into her hands, her blood mixing with his blood, bleach from the bucketwater clearing her knuckles of meat. *She keeps a nasty house and Lord knows*, she says, leaning closer to the faded stain until her lips nearly touch the ground, *no woman should live that way.*

Delicious, New Edition, 1986

You put the fire in my heart
boys sing and I swear
I'm their *taste of honey, girl*
every dream in me awakened.

Boys sing with flair,
look slick for the camera,
every dream awake and
alive. My parents,

in the thick of ruin, click the camera,
capturing me
like a sunrise, heir apparent,
on my way to my first concert.

They fracture me—
some parts mother, some father.
Soon, our first performance, our concert:
I will be five and cry as my parents scream.

Dressed like my father
in our fancy black and red
readied for five boys singing, my screaming:
tonight, we live for joy.

At home, our finery—starless, damp with sweat—
soon disappears.
Our living joy
shuttered like an aperture.

Soon we'll disappear
and what is harder to swallow:
joy, shuttered like an aperture
or the missing photographs, all that's captured, lost.

What hard act will follow
our broken record? No more us, just me and her and you.
Mother and I take the photographs, you miss what's captured,
soft, sweet nothings.

The record scratched in the move, skips, plays *you…you…*
my taste of honey, girl…
lost sweet nothings
you…the fire in my heart…delicious

Distant Lover

Dear Bobby: Cambodia, Vietnam, it's all on the news.
If I watch too long, the lines run together and
I can't tell who's who.

My sisters been my company,
especially Dee. We use an old map
to show the boys where you might be.

I listen to music, passing time.
Marvin's singing sweet in this new cut, he say
When your lover leaves you, you got nobody. A lonely hour's come over you.

He's live on stage, somewhere far like you
and those girls screaming behind him
must know he's telling the truth.

Remember that day we left the boys with my mama
when the bank gave us that loan?
The rain came down, drops big as pennies

and we didn't care, walked all the way home.
When we got back to Dunbar Street, we were a mess:
hair slick, clothes muddy, our shoes and hopes

in your hands and we just laughed.
People couldn't understand what it meant
to have someone believe in what we started.

We danced ourselves silly, soaked as we were
through and through—the rain came down like that today.
Days like this, I sure do miss you.

The Flock of Your Pasture

Who are the sons
        of the gods and their fury?

What weakness is given
        through fiber and blood?

Here is a boy I love,
        sixteen and filling in, who used to covet

miniatures, building farms or tiny zoos, herding them
        from room to room in their almost living.

He is a running back now, big cousin, fast as blame,
        Kool-aid smile on a hardening face.

Awakened one morning by arguing,
        his brother, sister and I

wait to be taken to the school bus.
        We know better than to interrupt

grown folks who tell us to run
        in another direction if a fight breaks out

but never mention our own houses,
        faces we kiss and carry,

arms that cradle us
        battering or bracing the other.

Forcing himself between his parents'
        wild cacophony, what choice does the boy have

but to learn to love by taking blows?
        His father shouting apologies,

his mother's indiscriminate swinging
        bruising the boy's chest and shoulders until

startled by the sight of him—something like
        a mirror shattering—

she drops her arms and passes out.
        How small he seems

in his inexperience, and how large
        growing into who he must become—

his face, like his father's,
        etched in thinly woven misery.

What shepherding can be done, what tending,
        when everyone has seen how much saving we'll need?

What will the boy carry
        besides the folded body of his mother?

What will he hold in the years to come
        but the weight of the heart in his hands?

Domestic

The doors have changed.
Where the wooden fence stood
a metal gate is latched.
The walkway and drive seem
too minute to have ever held us
and all our differences.

The eggshell house sits
across the cul-de-sac
and, there, the pick-up
I think I remember.
I almost expect to see
the blond woman ranting
from the front door
about our noise, our blackness,
then touting the neighborhood's
knowledge of our skeletons,
a bottle and half-empty
glass in her hand.

The house stands more vivid in memory
amidst flashing blue lights
after our faults
erupted between us—
the unwanted family
and the neighbor's wife
acting mistress, misfit,
misfiring against blood
and blood rushing her,
the women at war,
children yelling
obscenities from the door.

The house turned brighter
after the woman was
knocked to the ground
and finally retreated
after the police left
calling it *domestic*
taking no report.

And when it was well past
midnight, generations
sauntered through the house

recalling blows. How sweet it was
to pummel someone
who knew nothing of us,
to watch her sobering,
diminished—like the old house
loosed of our secrets—silent,
learned, spent through.

We Argue In Silence

I am another quiet morning.
He is one more early night.

We make a chasm in the creaking house
until the rift crashes over the bedroom

like a seismic wave. I wait
until we are poised for sleep

then bolt upright yelling
We're gonna stay up and fight tonight!

set to strike, but he will not do
what he is supposed to.

He refuses to raise his voice or hands.
He won't head for a bottle

or the street. He shakes his head, watching me
until I sit on my haunches

and tell him what's hurting.
I say, in bed, with my troubled sleep

This is a hard beginning
my back to him, the sheets spun tight

around my body, a partition.
He says   *Tomorrow*

we begin again
by pulling me in,

his arms wide
against the rustling.

Mary Robbins Dies 12 Days After Her Husband

Heart arrhythmia

                    the paper says

59 years of marriage

                    and everyone knows

what this means:

                    love can break you

or tie a slipknot

                    around the living

tethering

                    what blood can't:

the intangible

                    this strange breath

one giving life

                    one calling life back

II

Conduit

Science says we are not autonomous, we carry each other
in our bowels and bellies, in our brains.

Cells passed through birthing or breast milk
stay with our mothers,

their mothers; vespers that prove
we do not work of our own accord.

The miracle is: inside, we only give,
not like the taking that persists outside ourselves.

Foreign cells flurry to an injured heart
repairing it before ruin, staying

for years, tens of years, tens of thousands
if we kept on living as intended.

What I take from this is what we are reluctant to bear:
the whole world is nothing but a valley

and in that valley there are mountains made of trees
and trees made of grass and stars that fall into

the underbelly of everything beginning again.
How can all this be mistaken?

Who can imagine we are not made?
We save our memories and talents,

gristle and muscle and bone—
all of what we are—rescued and re-born.

In the womb there is the drum of the heart
beating, speaking to another small drum

and the music is a valley we are all coming to
conduits, chimeras, too vast to be named.

My Aunt Kisses Jackie Wilson

Aunt Shirley is telling the story again.
The girls were raging, guards were posted
near the stage but she was Olympic
and rushed him, Mr. Excitement singing
sweet, crooning she was the finest girl
he'd ever want to meet, and when she leapt
planting her hands, her hips, her pursed
lips, his silence was the record's groove
sidling up against another curve.
I believe in miracles and wonder,
so when she says he was prettier than any other
slick and moved like his body was anointed,
how he'd perfected the spiral and backbone
slip, I understand why she comes back
to the story, unrepentant, long after reproof,
why nothing—the broken years, the nonbelievers,
even the star's fall—halts the tailspin,
the way back when, when every
would-be wrong was right.
Her teardrops weren't caused
by the heart's lonesome pitching,
when the broken kiss was little more
than a new beginning. The spotlight gone
dark meant he could be waiting behind
some glittering door and everything
forbidden, everything desired, could be
new and renewed, at the encore.

Love In Stereo

I am almost convinced this morning by the volley
of verses on each frequency, roughnecks telling it

like they want it to be, intoning   *You bad, baby*
you know you wanna be with me   and who can resist prophecy?

Tough made pretty like pearl-handled switchblades,
their voices cut through airwaves, half-singing,

half-slinging pipeswinging and duress.
The ligature of bass and brash beckoning

might persuade anyone intent on believing
love is a hustler running game and lying tenderly.

Sex, a series of volatile incidents,
history of how we know we like it—slung

low and collective, wild for wild things.
My daughter adores the boy shaming and trilling:

Wonder if you're bending over backward for someone else,
doing things I taught you getting nasty for someone else?

But who should any listening girl be?
Not too devoted, just loose enough.

Never too black, too mouthy, too much.
What real thing does anyone want?

Who sings for the women I inherit?
Who hopes for a woman like me?

Spinning the dial, I wander
the netherworld of static cackling

until a beat that breaks my back each time
crosses the wire, hangs in the air like the men I'm carrying.

Vinyl

The last time I find myself
lying between the times
we make love, I run my fingers along
my own thigh in hopes that the door
will reopen, miraculous in its forgiveness,
its remarkable swing, its willingness, unlike mine

I can't keep looking at loneliness, trying to call it freedom

But when you re-enter, I have to rise
to meet you, clear the locks and bolts
meant to keep the safe distance I pledged.
These are the times I think of my mother—
her bitter duty—the nights my father
ambled back toward us. His reverent
silence, her reluctant undoing—
the fastened chain swinging open

I can't keep looking at loneliness, trying to call it freedom

This history we call love is no longer a remedy.
I refuse you, as you have me for spite, little else.
All night, you beckon from the other side
of the door, but I hear only my father's voice—
muffled, full of regret for the irreparable—
the skipping record, the needle's worn slide.

I can't keep looking at loneliness, trying to call it freedom

Scene

This is the storyline unchanged:
the foreground is a woman's house
which I will come to love
forty years from now
when I have aged and been born,
when a man has remedied the woman's
wounds after another has nearly
murdered her, with all the careless
world and neighbors watching.
The reckless man hits the woman
and the unborn come
running, tucked beneath
the arms and eyelids
of our mothers, her sisters,
storming the porch
to save the innocents
nearly lost in the house's bleeding.

The climax is the gun:
and endless fingers clamoring
for the trigger. This is the story
they tell when one of us
is cracked open, left
a discolored bruise.
And if I know anything at all
it's the character of that summer night
when every generation learned
how to end love, how to free it
with the threat of a bullet,
how to leave a man
in an empty corner, stained
and trembling, remembering
the denouement—the barrel
pressed to his temple
and every eye in the warm night air
turned blind and cold.

Getting Ready for the Heartache to Come or A Body Intercepting Light

>   Ps. 39:6 – *Surely every man walks about like a shadow.*

Grief is a half-sung ballad
>   the mothers I've known are bellowing

into stilled ears or stitches
>   in the sewn up backs of blue-black boys.

There are various sites of trauma:
>   wombs, needles, pipes, badges,

ropes unraveling, all wavelengths of visible light,
>   prison fights, the Devil's busy hands.

Bodies aimed when they leave
>   like bullets or planes, rarely become letters,

tulips, fireworks, any welcome opening,
>   rarely live as good, as free, as long

as we hope. The women enduring this
>   must become: saints or blameworthy,

miracles or memories. The Bible says men
>   are gods or gleaning but mothers shelter

the in-between: ghost-children wandering the streets
>   of every generation—father-god, son-god, holy-

spirit—flexing in photo albums, toys in the curio,
>   lighters, guns and flasks carved

with initials, all the left-behind things
>   gathered around a table, mothers

singing, *Didn't I do the best I could, didn't I?*

Lactation Room

When a woman in my workshop brings her breast pump
to the counter, we have to find the Lactation Room
in the library so she can create
what her child will need.
The girls at the Information Desk are perplexed,
Which place? I've never heard of that.
They squint and scour a multicolor map.
I've seen the closed door
on the second floor but I, too,
must imagine what's there.
Maybe a cedar table like the one in the lobby,
a pillow soft couch, a rocking chair?
Pictures of breasts or babies
on the wall, like in my gynecologist's office,
charts and models or maybe artistic nudes
like in the restroom at my favorite brasserie.
How do the women know how long to remain—
do they stop when it aches or go to relieve the aching?
What choices do they make
to allow for this, what are they given
in the spaces leading to such mystery—
an unbound gift or hardship? In the end,
I draw a diagram clearer than
the map heavy with distance,
and off the mother goes
into the unknown,
the girls, a bit wiser,
and I, still
in wonder.

How I Knew Michael

Around 1993 my best friend is defying her mother again. She loves his cousin, older and too wise. We are their diversions. His voice is deep and scolding. He tells me not to pine after Reggie, he's trouble. Years later, when I hear Reggie's killed a man, I'll remember he was right.

Around 2009 he seeks me out. We are of different worlds—I write and cling to the ocean, he works and raises children. When he finds me, I'm as happy as I've ever been, poeming mountains, counting my stars. His children tell me they know my name, all their lives they've said it from afar.

Around 1976 his mother leaves her parents' house. She's met his father and found another difficult home.

Around 1981 we are born, one in winter, one in spring. We are both miracles, we are both burdens. We grow up fast trying not to get in the way of things.

Around 1997 I leave Phoenix and won't apologize for shunning him in the eighth grade, turning to salt and stone. This troubles me but I go on.

Around 1958 our mothers are made or being made, our fathers are thought of or have tumbled in, all ready, wreaking havoc, not knowing what will become of them.

Around 1994 he kisses me at a roller rink, then behind a theater we should be inside of. We will be caught. He'll still taste sweet.

Around 1999 we'll both hate what formed us: necessity, impatience, love. This anger carries us: he becomes reckless, I learn to hold a mean grudge.

Around 1977 my father spies my mother in a frame while he's visiting Aunt Shirley and Uncle Bobby's place. They all ride with a CB Club and daddy's the deejay. He sees her captured there and believes she's all he'll ever want to know. When she comes to the pool in a yellow two-piece, he decides how soon he'll propose.

Around 2009 we laugh all night. The sun sets through his window and rises through mine. *You're such a good friend,* I tell him. *Is that what you think I want you for?* he says *You're my wife.* I hold the line.

***Regents Prompt: What are the best ways for step-parents to deal
with the special problems they face?***

To harbor nothing.
To leave this earth without anything
hovering over you—no angels

or demons, flowerless. Waking easily in the morning
means more rivalry with no one but you—the divine quiet deafening.
See a child being born if you are able;

fear is a deterrent against harm. Touch
another breathing thing, you'll surely run the risk of marrying,
bound by the weight you'll cradle.

*

Bound by the weight, you'll cradle
another breathing thing. You'll surely run the risk of marrying
fear. Is a deterrent against harm touch?

See, a child being born—if you are Abel—
means more rivalry. With no one but you (the Divine), quiet (deafening)
or demons (flowerless) wake easily. In the morning,

hovering over you, no angels.
To leave this earth without anything
to harbor. Nothing.

East River Drive

Paved with starlight and error
        those Augusta hills held
                what little we'd save.
                        Red clay flaring

as we coursed the highway
        or settled into the driveway
                of the house soon to be taken,
                      lost to the needle's

sharp misery. There was always
        the sound of the black and white
                cassette rewound until
                      our street was *East River Drive*

my father, the melancholy horn,
        my mother, somewhere behind
                the snare. I kept time
                      in the seat next to her

as we searched, hoping
        to find someone other
                than who we knew would appear:
                      a stranger

pretending he hadn't gone
        missing, that there was nothing
                extraordinary about him,
                      that the melody—

queued and replayed—
        wasn't a warning there'd be
                many more nights like this,
                      that the road would be so long.

The Lift

It stops for no one

we stand on a yellow square
at the ride's entrance
and wait to be taken

gliding over the big top
over the food stands' commingling air
we brace for when we might disembark
leave the lift's slow tilt

its wires coursed above
the world tethered
to the entrance
to the path that led
here past our inhibitions
into almost heaven

where we reveal how the years
have fixed or ruined us
how we are fearful of descent
the way breath can be
taken at will

and no warning
no sign blaring *Exit*
in the far off distance
can ground us

III

Counsel, Wedding Day

Say, *I lied.*
        Say, *It wasn't your fault.*
Laugh in bed.
        Laugh in the shower.
Laugh as you walk in the rain.
        Start out like you can hold out.
Don't expect what you won't give.
        Repeat grandma's refrain –
        Courtin' is a pretty thing, marriage is a blossom.
        If you want to get your finger bit,
        poke it at a possum.
Shake your heads and smile.
        Don't wound on purpose.
Put a dimmer in.
        Slide around the kitchen
        in stockings and dress socks.
Make it a dance.
        Sing when he asks.
Clean when she asks.
        Pray about weaknesses.
Know you are not God
and can change nothing.
        Buy those sweets he likes.
Feed that man.
        Remember.
Hold hands.
        Let old records play.

Bend, don't break.

    Keep folks out your marriage.

Bind the three-fold cord.

    Give her shoes and compliments.

Buy dirty magazines;

leave pictures,

by way of instruction.

    Don't be afraid

      to wear him out.

Forgive. Forgive. Forgive.

    Consider it all joy.

Equal Measure

Daughters teach you everything.
I know this

but still ask my husband if he can
braid my hair

because he's been away
from his daughter

nine months now
and is sick with idleness.

We are in the kitchen,
 I've just returned from a trip—

three more nights he's learned
to live alone—

and my hair is one large mess
nothing like his daughter's

in the school picture
after hours of clips and combs and care.

Just as he has always said it,
he says *Yes* while I part

two equal measures then condition
the length, make it easier to tame.

He stands beside me, patient
as the waiting season.

When he suffers the mass,
fashioning thick plaits, he says

lean and *please*
and some words in between but

I am taken up by the tenderness
of him, his hands

most like those of familiar
women, learned and unafraid.

In bed, we dream of different things—
I am covered in a flurry

of his warm skin. All night
he is collecting dolls,

beads, little shoes;
he is worn thin

with searching.
In the morning

after I've given him
so little room

to sleep—my body at rest only
when pressed in odd curvature against his—

I find his work
has survived

and, as I haven't learned yet
to bear all his undoing,

I comb out the plaits but leave
their waves and impressions—

my hair, full as when I was a girl,
its art, filled with his sorrows.

Fast Car

Tracy sang   *Maybe we'll make something*
as my father and I drove townships, studying songs
divining anywhere could be a kind of home.

Even Red Bank, past Cherry Street, Gus' Barbershop
and the Chinese eatery we ordered from most nights that summer
he spent showing me remnants of the place I was born.

In the green and white house (that burned down in autumn)
the music is all we had for sure, so the fire was a mercy
taking no sound just things.

After the divorce, there were a thousand miles between us.
Strange to see Daddy making ends meet all alone—
doing odd jobs and shopping at the corner store,

sweeping the shag carpet, haggard and orange.
It wasn't a pretty place but city lights laid out before us
and we sang in unison learning what the other loved most.

We couldn't salvage everything—I never found
my unbroken self, never asked what he lost
by losing me, what he'd suffered to remember.

When my mother would call, to soothe her
in the distance, I'd mention what we'd seen:
the base housing we lived in before

our orders to Germany, Triple S Bar
on Route 35 where the CB Club used to meet.
She needn't worry; he hadn't lost everything.

There were still pictures of her
in his wallet, crates of albums and cassettes,
some he'd let me keep.

His voice was a fire and my inheritance
traveling dirt roads and overseas—the engine
of longing, a tuned and mended piece of me.

To outsiders, it must have seemed
like the whole heap of us had been destroyed
but some people save themselves

by driving on, leaving what's left as kindling.
That summer the fire in us passed back and forth
was a clearing, an offering to be consumed

until every room was filled with music
in the days before the house
burned down.

We Awaken Near the Ocean After Being Married

I am spark or light, you are bead

of salt and hum and teeth.

Clay and ash transformed to

stone and ore, fever slick

enraptured, born and re-born.

The ear to the ground in our room

finds one wild bruising art—

hunger and bellyful, fully-fleshed.

What I know for sure is the heart

is like the sea with its dark urging:

wide over everything, breathless and breaking.

Son·sor·éa (\sahn-soar-ray\)

        Luminary of questions

   formed from dust and inexperience.

Daughter of Sonia and Michael

    who now, by fate, has come to me.

        Reluctant bridge bearing the weight

            of her untraceable name.

      How could we have known

         which planets would collide

              and give rise to one who'd stray

        the paths of our roaming,

    boundless, growing wild, demanding

an answer for what's always asked.

        Everyone wants to know how

    to pronounce it, what it means.

It begins like a song we keep trying to sing

     then ends in beckoning, like most things

        we dream but can't pin down.

            Code for *angle-voiced taunter of brother,*

laundry avoider, lover of saccharine and sleep,

              synonym for teenager,

        derivative of *in medias res*—

   molding clay or cloudy mirror—

bird in want of nest and air.

It could mean *ray of the sun* in some native tongue,
what we've held thus far,
but more likely is   *young heart that yearns toward you,*
boyish, uncertain, like the myriad of us
given time to learn what we love.

We are tied together like this
in odd and fortunate symmetry:
our names invented, infinite
like the journey entire.
And what passage doesn't teach
each of us, stitched like a jagged seam—

and couldn't that be what it means: *all we haven't lost*
or broken, the possible gained?—

then, no matter how we arrive,
by what force or where or when,
who wouldn't remember
it was always beautiful?

Ways to Please a Five-year-old Superhero

Don't call him The Blur. Do teach him to spell it.
Play the fastest breakbeat you can find,
watch him as he dances.
Tell him he's a master
and no one's close to keeping up.
Explain fish scales, shadows,
ocean waves, and underwear
when he asks about their purpose.
Kiss his father in the kitchen
at the sink. Kiss both his cheeks
next. Say   *You were right*
that time   when he argues with his sister.
Buy toy cars in red and yellow metal.
Leave them in a shiny bag
on his bed. Let him sit
in the 'man chair' upstairs,
though it often swallows him when he rocks.
When he gives you dandelions
pretend they are irises.
When he misses the toilet
applaud him for making it
to the bathroom.
If he wants to climb
in your lap, all arms and eyelashes,
give him a leg up; don't squirm
when his elbow skewers your ribs.
Serve drumsticks for dinner,
hide the vegetables in the rice.
He'll say   *You're the best*
cooker I know   if you've done it right.
Let him run in the house.
Try not to yell about steps and corners.
When he asks   *Am I good*
at being good?   Tell him
though he's wiggling from his seat
with stained hands and shirttail wagging
he's the strongest, he's the fastest, he's the best.

Baby Be Mine

The song is honeymint
on his tongue. In his sleep

he answers questions—
There'll be no more mountains

and gives commands—
Make sweet love this way.

Blind root worker
making turnstiles of us

as I wake, he spins into my hollows
half-dreaming

and when good sense plagues me—
fear of what could be—

he is still beside me, singing
As long as we believe.

Noble & Webster, Shadow Sculptures

      There are illusions stacked into a kind of mortality:
out front, all the unwanted creation
          left to tell the stories. Behind the rubble

      calculated coupling: a man and woman
in shadow. A glass held to his mouth, her fraying thread—
          all makeshift fashioning

      which teaches us:
everything overlooked and worn
          can be turned into something useful.

      Our house is a mess of musk and sawdust—
things others have given away—keels and scrim and kin
          caught in the net of our limbs.

      In the sculpture, there are gulls wide-winged and famished,
peanut butter containers, aluminum cans,
          a broken measuring tape made new, things we forget

      to see each day that prove:
one house can become many houses,
          one room many rooms,

      one womb an ugly
kind of living, still life,
          cast in the right light.

Solstice

When you discover you are old enough
that nothing has novelty

you live with teenagers
who've learned

little more than to abhor everything—*I hate Daylight Savings Time.*
I hate Virginia. I hate being here.

They hate that the dark comes on early
and wonder what other secrets

we've been keeping
on this side of the world.

If we can steal their light and time
without warning

what joy is there to be had,
what can they love without fear?

What else will we reveal
in the quick of an hour,

the shortened days,
all their hurried years?

Skipping Stones

Children aren't forced to love you and you aren't forced to love them;
we all have the right to say exactly what we mean.

So when the child spits   *You're not my mom anyway*
you are all at once given the gift of enlightenment

remembering your mother's rage as you slammed
the door she paid for, barely that month,

working double shifts and hiding rent
money in her bra or Bible

and the humiliation of your father
after, in front of your giggling girlfriends—

one whose father sold him dope and one
whose father was using too—you threw

the truth at him   *You're not mom*
so you can't tell me what to do

and he smacked you across the face
then went and cried for a long time in his room.

When your station is hurled like a river stone
there are very few options to choose:

swallow it in one way or another
or, if you are fearless, knowing

no child has ever learned
by anything other than mimicry,

cast it back onto the wavering surface
into the wide mouths always coming.

IV

Training or a Weapon

When I am ten, months before my father teaches me patiently, my uncle throws me into the pool's deep end yelling *Sink or swim!* like the Marine he will always be. I sputter and falter like a flooded engine. His hands smack the water. I claw at the edge of intricate design until I am angry and alive. He briefs his children and me, as I am the fifth child he must carry, on what has been drilled into him: sometimes the body must be broken to endure. He is a damaged child, though he thinks we don't know it, have forgotten perhaps, the stories told when he leaves a room. We all trace the scars of his body silently each time he enters the pool. I am as much his daughter as another's. He is as much a son as the boy I'm raising, as my father was, as all the boys are to the ones they're left to. My uncle is as loud as I imagine combat would be, saving me, when I am in the Atlantic with my children, one stroke short of breathing, his lesson—*Sink or swim!*—rushing back like a wartime memory. Baptism by fire, fear or love, whatever it was, we wouldn't reach the shore without it. That push into some uncertain end reminding us the elements—like parents and lovers and orders—are just another arm of God to pass through.

On Religion

We wait until we are wed to make love because God knows the body better than us. We've broken our bodies in the past using irons, razors, swing sets, steep steps, lovers and careless piety. We are responsible for these injuries. We don't want to hurt each other, and this is enough to keep us chaste. Jehovah is first but in the second place there's this contempt we share for those who tell us what we will never do. Someone once told him, his quiet was a ruining, someone once told me *You'll never spare as much of yourself as anyone needs—this* is a god he carries, *that* a god who carries me. There are legions we are trying to exorcise and abyss—gods of brutal hunger, gods of our silencing, gods of the closed-fisted, gods of impossibility.

Photograph

The mouth holds
a scar that trails the temple

cheek and chin of a man
sometimes called father.

And when the man spoke
even in his right mind

my husband recalls
he'd rehash old warnings:

I told you, you were going to hate me
after the mother or child

climbed the mountain
of his frame settling

near enough destruction
to trace its inward part.

Our child is not yet ten and we are clearing his closet

of do-rags, backpacks, hoodoo, hoorides, black
magic, mysterious gadgets, misters and missus, the missing,
heretics, hearsay, heard-him-tell, run-and-tell-it,
snitches, stitches, stichs, saving, saviors, Toms, Dicks,
nightsticks, shanks, broken bottles, blunts, objects,
bullets, ballistics, crypt walks, autopsies, undergrounds,
jaywalking, gestures, gentrification, justifications, juries,
kickbacks, nickelbags, accessories, neverseen, dragging, drug
cartels, trafficking, riding while, driving while, looking while,
loudtalking, Mirandas, bandanas, the ash faultline,
blood in the streets, Bloods in these streets, gang-
banging, bass slanging, Ma-we-was-just-out-listening-to
at the wrong place, wrong time, tongue-tying, art-
iculation, relations, bad association, watch who you
know, love, bump into, fistbumping, fist fighting, forced
arrest, urban unrest, what it looks like, who coins it,
who sets up camp, who's pictured on those shirts,
why children are in these streets, what blisters
and buoys, *Boy, tie up those laces, unzip that hood*

We See *The Lion King* on Broadway, I Enter the Pride

Our girl is telling the boys to pose near the theater doors.
We have traveled to the Minskoff in New York

and the children are finally elated.
They have been trying to teach me

their ways—they wrestle and weary one another,
bending and binding love—but I am useless in my tenderness

until this: I have orchestrated the daytrip of dreams.
Herald Square gleams like a lost enchantress.

As we scuttle and preen, she tries pashminas and caps,
designer shades, everything neon at once. When our tickets have been taken

and they step into the circle, for a flash of moment,
she takes the journey in. It is only a measure

before the music starts, while we head to our seats,
she says   *This is amazing—*

*all you've done to get us here. It must have taken
hours.* Years, I think, years, but she is grateful

and I am finally useful. As the curtain goes up,
everything the light touches is ours.

Some Sorrow, Some Joy

In the photograph
we have made it out
of the eighth grade, together.

He's spent most of the year
missing laughter and sleep,
barely breathing.

This is the year he trusts
his father and realizes his mistake
like other setbacks

with the appearance of
necessity—quick-footed,
childish things.

The same year I stop hoping
my parents will remember
their gravity

more than what detritus
pried us free, and I hurt
everyone near me.

This is the sorrow:
understanding come too late,
and I can do nothing now but

let him retell the forsaking
a few times each season, whenever
we visit the children's classrooms

since it seems to make him
visible in the haze
of those lost and wandering years.

The mercy is
that joy comes soon after,
as we are, just this morning,

twenty years from that moment
and still holding each other
in the music-laced dark.

Well into night
we laugh at our recollections
of cousins and old friends

who are part of us
that we'll pray for and forget to call
or avoid calling

in the busy pattern of
our continuous unfolding
we've gained and hold dear,

this history
we can't unravel
and wouldn't if we could.

A student writes the thesis: *If you never find your soulmate, this is when one must face the harsh reality of making major decisions alone* **and, though the grammar is incorrect, I give him credit**

My husband enters
each morning

holding two shirts and ties,
sometimes wearing

different shoes. The brown or
the dark brown?

Hat or no hat? Khaki or coal?
Which one? he asks

and I tell him all I know.

    *

I read aloud to him,
Baldwin, Anaïs Nin,

the lines I mostly remember
others forget. I ask

Isn't that beautiful?
and he tells me I am beautiful.

I go to my desk
poised with all I know.

If this world is ending

All I've been meaning to say is: I was wrong

when we were children and you knew

to love me like we'd end up in each other's arms.

And I was the foolish one, who thought God couldn't

make anything possible and wouldn't

move space and time to bring us into being.

Without me, you might not have wasted those years

on doubt. Without me, you may have been

granted every gladness in between.

But here we are now—root and bud

and grafting—me with my regrets

and you with your believing:

great deity of all mending,

surest light I've ever known.

Beckoning

        They name him Christian.

They see him in others, in my arms.

        They wonder about his eyes and ears.

        They bargain: *What about next year? What about when we're not so broke?*

They point out the silver lining: love after love after love.

        They beg.

        They enlist my mother.

That is an inaccuracy; they align themselves

        with my mother.

They lose their patience, get indignant.

        They talk to him at the dinner table.

        They set a place.

They count the years between them.

        Sometimes, they are good and quiet as a trap.

        They leave off for a while but always come back.

They call the barren, the broken, the distant well-worn.

        They are the living beckoning the unborn.

Mother Necessity

He is concerned about the way words work
if his sister will be angry, if his father will.

He asks me over homework
if I've talked to them again.

I tell him no one minds the word *mom* around here.
But that's what I call my real Mom too   he says

What if it gets confused?
It won't, I tell him, she and I are never

in the same place at the same time.
He tries it out in a rhyme—*Be calm, mom*—

when he is late to bed
or early morning howling up the stairs

and sometimes I forget
who I've become.

What a strange life this is: in part, who you think you are
but mostly what others deem.

Nameless, then newly named,
ghost of someone's dreams.

To Her Whose Heart Is My Heart's Quiet Home

Mother: do you remember the crystal vase
broken in the move to Germany

or was it in your first loud argument,
what must have felt like penance,

for marrying too soon a man who loves you now
like he has been carved of your hands?

I've forgotten to thank you for never teaching me
to hate entirely, just remember what fires

swept into the field can ruin
—every seedling, every bulb—

and who of us could explain
refusing to save some?

When that vase fractured
into the innumerable

you could have ended things,
snatched your baby and your albums—

riddled as they were with imprints of another—
but you stayed to tend the smoldering.

We are your handiwork:
these generations you've taught

what to cut away, what to keep.
Your lover—the salvaged kindling,

and me and mine—like crystal
made whole and sparkling.

Starlight Park

I invited him there
        when we were twelve
for the Memorial of the death of Christ.
        We were children,
trussed and aimed by other hands
        but odd in our maturity.
We spent hours on the phone
        dissecting sex and theorems and history.
Who's to say we weren't
        ions of matter—
the phenomena
        coupled by gravity?
He and I in the creaking seats
        near our mothers acknowledging each other,
our fathers in their orbits
        circling home.
Could we see God there
        in that school auditorium—
unsuspecting holy place—
        one transfigured into another,
how sometimes we are bigger
        than our mistakes?
What was born?   We couldn't name it,
        just listened, passed bread and wine.
Were we sent into being
        without warning that night,
in the world spinning despite our destruction,
        were we fixed,
did we burst and collide?

Notes

The book's epigraph is taken from Julia B. Levine's poem "Netherland".

"If It's Magic" takes its title from a song on Stevie Wonder's album *Songs in the Key of Life*.

"Distant Lover" take their title from a song on *Marvin Gaye Live!* released in 1974. The first poem owes deference to the book *Bloods: An Oral History of the Vietnam War* by Black Veterans by Wallace Terry. The second poem utilizes dialogue Marvin Gaye spoke to an audience of screaming fans before launching into his performance of the song.

"Young, small, and growing, often violently" takes its title from a NASA news article entitled "Hubble Goes to the eXtreme to Assemble Farthest-Ever View of the Universe" found on www.nasa.gov.

"Delicious, New Edition, 1986" takes its title from a song on New Edition's self-titled album.

"The Flock of Your Pasture" is written for Rodney Williams and takes its title from Psalm 79:13 in the *New World Translation of the Holy Scriptures* (2013) published by the Watchtower Bible and Tract Society. All other scriptural quotes in this work are from this translation as well.

"Mary Robbins Dies 12 Days After Her Husband" takes its title from an article on *Yahoo! News*.

"Conduit" is based on an article published in *Scientific American* entitled "Scientists Discover Children's Cells Living in Mothers' Brains".

"My Aunt Kisses Jackie Wilson" is written after Reginald Shepherd's poem "My Mother Dated Otis Redding".

"Love In Stereo" uses lines from the song "Hotline Bling" on Drake's album *Views*.

"Vinyl" takes its refrain from the song "I Want to Spend the Night" on Bill Wither's album *Menagerie*.

"Getting Ready for the Heartache to Come or A Body Intercepting Light" takes part of its title and final line from the song "Standing in the Shadows of Love" on the Four Tops' album *Reach Out*.

"Lactation Room" is written for Jenifer Alonzo.

"How I Knew Michael" is written after Deborah Harding's poem "How I Knew Harold".

"East River Drive" takes its title from a song on Grover Washington, Jr.'s album *Come Morning*

"Fast Car" takes its title from a song on Tracy Chapman's self-titled album and uses several phrases from the song.

"Baby Be Mine" takes its title from a song on Michael Jackson's album *Thriller*.

"Training or a Weapon" takes its title from lines in Sharon Olds' poem "Indictment of Senior Officers".

"Mother Necessity" takes its title from a song included in the *Schoolhouse Rock!* animated series.

"To Her Whose Heart Is My Heart's Quiet Home" takes its title from a line in Christina Rossetti's poem that begins "[Sonnets are full of love, and this my tome]".

Acknowledgments

Grateful acknowledgment is given to the following publications where some of these poems first appeared, sometimes in different versions or under different titles: "East River Drive," *Weave*; "My Aunt Kisses Jackie Wilson," *Weave* and *Library of Congress, The Poet and the Poem Radio Program*; "How I Knew Michael," *Pluck!*; "Cleaning House," *PoemMemoirStory*; "Domestic," *Huizache*; "A student writes the thesis: If you never find your soulmate, this is when one must face the harsh reality of making major decisions alone and, though the grammar is incorrect, I give him credit," *Hauser's Jewelers Juror's Prize*; "Fast Car," *Affilia*; "If It's Magic," *Ploughshares*; "We Argue in Silence," *Ithaca Lit*; "Young, small and growing, often violently," *Common Ground Review*; "Son·sor·éa (\sahn-soar-ray\)," *Poems and Their Making: A Conversation*; "Baby Be Mine," "Equal Measure" and "Ways to Please a Five-year-old Superhero," *Grace Cavalieri's Featured Poets* (danmurano.com); "Our child is not yet ten and we are clearing his closet" and "Conduit," *Fjords Review*; "Scene," *MiPoesias*, nominated for a 2016 *Pushcart Prize*; "Mary Robbins Dies 12 Days After Her Husband," *Tuesday; An Art Project*; "The Flock of Your Pasture," *Hunger Mountain*; and "Benediction," "We Awaken Near the Ocean After Being Married" and "If this world is ending," *Diode Poetry Journal*.

All praise to Jehovah God for inspiring 1 John 4:7—"Beloved ones, let us continue loving one another, because love is from God, and everyone who loves has been born from God and knows God."

Mom, Daddy, Aunt Shirley, Uncle Bobby: Everything I've come to know is born through the love of you.

I am forever indebted to my husband and children and thank them for this gift. My Cute Sweet Man: you are the love of my life; thank you for walking in faith with me. Sonsoréa, Johnathan and Big Michael #2: you teach me something new each waking moment, but most of all that love is remembering the sacrifice it has taken to get us here. Sonia: thank you for trust.

All my love to my family, the Bingham, Knight, Anderson clans, and all other extended villages, especially to the women of the family who are mirrors, however large or small, for me: Alesia Anderson, Shirley Bingham, Loretta Bingham, Robin Hardy, Rosalind Ellington, Deborah Bingham, Kalani Dozier, Yolanda Bingham, Mary Brown, Carolyn Wyatt, Eunice Eubanks, Annette Knight, Deborah Anderson, Sherry Knight, Patricia Brown, Darveen Jordan, Delanya Hoskins, Lenika Hill, Bernice Anderson, Lawanda Anderson, Judy Reese-Callaway and Phyllis Smith. To Robbie Jr., Rodney, Ryan and Richelle Williams: for being as close as brothers and my only sister.

To those who were my babies for many years before—thank you for never being too old to come back to me: Jasmin Francis, Shavon Johnson, Rashad Williams and Nicole Reid.

So many mentors and friends helped carry me through the journey of this book—deep gratitude and love to: the wide net that is Cave Canem, the Affrilachian Poets, Matilda Cox and Princess Joy L. Perry (Road Dawgs extraordinaire), Tim Seibles (for all his belief),

L. Lamar Wilson (who believes love is revolutionary and reminds me of such), Christian Campbell, Honorée Fanonne Jeffers, Eugene Calloway, Laurie Cannady, Amanda Johnston, Dante Micheaux, Reginald Dwayne Betts, Myron Michael Hardy, Jeannie and Travis Kim-McPherson (who remind me what love is supposed to look like), Anita Darcel Taylor, Ada Udechukwu, Randall Horton, Rachel Eliza Griffiths, Diane Raptosh, Starr Troup, A. Van Jordan, Patricia Spears Jones, Grace Cavalieri, and Natasha Taylor and Monica Black: who both encourage me by always holding out hope for words to come.

A special thank you to Patty Paine and Law Alsobrook at Diode Editions, for saying love was necessary, and for all their care.

To all those who continually sustain me: light and love.